THE KING'S THRESHOLD

1904

By W. B. YEATS

In Memory of
Frank Fay
and his beautiful speaking in the
character of Seanchan

A Digireads.com Book
Digireads.com Publishing

The King's Threshold
By W. B. Yeats
ISBN 10: 1-4209-4166-6
ISBN 13: 978-1-4209-4166-1

Please visit *www.digireads.com*

PERSONS IN THE PLAY

King Guaire

Seanchan (pronounced Shanahan)

His Pupils

The Mayor of Kinvara

Two Cripples

Brian, an old servant

The Lord High Chamberlain

A Soldier

A Monk

Court Ladies

Two Princesses

Fedelm

Steps before the Palace of King Guaire at Gort. A table or litter in front of steps at one side, with food on it, and a bench. Seanchan lying on steps. Pupils before steps. King on the upper step before a curtained door.

KING. I welcome you that have the mastery
    Of the two kinds of Music: the one kind
    Being like a woman, the other like a man.
    Both you that understand stringed instruments,
    And how to mingle words and notes together
    So artfully that all the Art's but Speech
    Delighted with its own music: and you that carry
    The twisted horn, and understand the notes
    That lacking words escape Time's chariot;
    For the high angels that drive the horse of Time—
    The golden one by day, by night the silver—
    Are not more welcome to one that loves the world
    For some fair woman's sake.
    I have called you hither
    To save the life of your great master, Seanchan,
    For all day long it has flamed up or flickered
    To the fast-cooling hearth.

OLDEST PUPIL. When did he sicken?
    Is it a fever that is wasting him?

KING. No fever or sickness. He has chosen death:
    Refusing to eat or drink, that he may bring
    Disgrace upon me; for there is a custom,
    An old and foolish custom, that if a man
    Be wronged, or think that he is wronged, and starve
    Upon another's threshold till he die,
    The common people, for all time to come,
    Will raise a heavy cry against that threshold,
    Even though it be the King's.

OLDEST PUPIL. My head whirls round;
    I do not know what I am to think or say.
    I owe you all obedience, and yet

How can I give it, when the man I have loved
More than all others, thinks that he is wronged
So bitterly that he will starve and die
Rather than bear it? Is there any man
Will throw his life away for a light issue?

KING. It is but fitting that you take his side
    Until you understand how light an issue
    Has put us by the ears. Three days ago
    I yielded to the outcry of my courtiers—
    Bishops, Soldiers, and Makers of the Law—
    Who long had thought it against their dignity
    For a mere man of words to sit amongst them
    At the great council of the State and share
    In their authority. I bade him go,
    Though at the first with kind and courteous words,
    But when he pleaded for the poets' right,
    Established at the establishment of the world,
    I said that I was King, and that all rights
    Had their original fountain in some king,
    And that it was the men who ruled the world,
    And not the men who sang to it, who should sit
    Where there was the most honour. My courtiers—
    Bishops, Soldiers, and Makers of the Law—
    Shouted approval; and amid that noise
    Seanchan went out, and from that hour to this,
    Although there is good food and drink beside him,
    Has eaten nothing.

OLDEST PUPIL. I can breathe again.
    You have taken a great burden from my mind,
    For that old custom's not worth dying for.

KING. Persuade him to eat or drink. Till yesterday
    I thought that hunger and weakness had been enough;
    But finding them too trifling and too light
    To hold his mouth from biting at the grave,
    I called you hither, and all my hope's in you,
    And certain of his neighbours and good friends
    That I have sent for. While he is lying there,
    Perishing there, my good name in the world
    Is perishing also. I cannot give way,
    Because I am King; because, if I give way,
    My nobles would call me a weakling, and, it may be,
    The very throne be shaken.

OLDEST PUPIL. I will persuade him.
Your words had been enough persuasion, King;
But being lost in sleep or reverie,
He cannot hear them.

KING. Make him eat or drink.
Nor is it all because of my good name
I'd have him do it, for he is a man
That might well hit the fancy of a king,
Banished out of his country, or a woman's
Or any other's that can judge a man
For what he is. But I that sit a throne,
And take my measure from the needs of the State,
Call his wild thought that overruns the measure,
Making words more than deeds, and his proud will
That would unsettle all, most mischievous,
And he himself a most mischievous man.

[*He turns to go, and then returns again.*]

Promise a house with grass and tillage land,
An annual payment, jewels and silken wear,
Or anything but that old right of the poets.

[*He goes into palace.*]

OLDEST PUPIL. The King did wrong to abrogate our right;
But Seanchan, who talks of dying for it,
Talks foolishly. Look at us, Seanchan;
Waken out of your dream and look at us,
Who have ridden under the moon and all the day,
Until the moon has all but come again,
That we might be beside you.

SEANCHAN [*half turning round, leaning on his elbow, and speaking as if in a dream*].
I was but now
In Almhuin, in a great high-raftered house,
With Finn and Osgar. Odours of roast flesh
Rose round me, and I saw the roasting spits;
And then the dream was broken, and I saw
Grania dividing salmon by a stream.

OLDEST PUPIL. Hunger has made you dream of roasting flesh;
    And though I all but weep to think of it,
    The hunger of the crane, that starves himself
    At the full moon because he is afraid
    Of his own shadow and the glittering water,
    Seems to me little more fantastical
    Than this of yours.

SEANCHAN. Why, that's the very truth.
    It is as though the moon changed everything—
    Myself and all that I can hear and see;
    For when the heavy body has grown weak,
    There's nothing that can tether the wild mind
    That, being moonstruck and fantastical,
    Goes where it fancies. I have even thought
    I knew your voice and face, but now the words
    Are so unlikely that I needs must ask
    Who is it that bids me put my hunger by.

OLDEST PUPIL. I am your oldest pupil, Seanchan;
    The one that has been with you many years—
    So many that you said at Candlemas
    I had almost done with school, and all but knew
    Every thing that's known of poetry.

SEANCHAN. My oldest pupil? No, that cannot be,
    For it is some one of the courtly crowds
    That have been round about me from sunrise,
    And I am tricked by dreams; but I'll refute them.
    At Candlemas I bid that pupil tell me
    Why poetry is honoured, wishing to know
    If he had any weighty argument
    For distant countries and strange, churlish kings.
    What did he answer?

OLDEST PUPIL. I said the poets hung
    Images of the life that was in Eden
    About the child-bed of the world, that it,
    Looking upon those images, might bear
    Triumphant children. But why must I stand here,
    Repeating an old lesson, while you starve?

SEANCHAN. Tell on, for I begin to know the voice.
    What evil thing will come upon the world
    If the Arts perish?

OLDEST PUPIL. If the Arts should perish,
    The world that lacked them would be like a woman
    That, looking on the cloven lips of a hare,
    Brings forth a hare-lipped child.

SEANCHAN. But that's not all:
    For when I asked you how a man should guard
    Those images, you had an answer also,
    If you're the man that you have claimed to be,
    Comparing them to venerable things
    God gave to men before He gave them wheat.

OLDEST PUPIL. I answered—and the word was half your own—
    That he should guard them as the Men of Dea
    Guard their four treasures, as the Grail King guards
    His holy cup, or the pale, righteous horse
    The jewel that is underneath his horn,
    Pouring out life for it as one pours out
    Sweet heady wine. . . . But now I understand;
    You would refute me out of my own mouth;
    And yet a place at council, near the King,
    Is nothing of great moment, Seanchan.
    How does so light a thing touch poetry?

        [Seanchan is now sitting up. He still looks dreamily in front of him.]

SEANCHAN. At Candlemas you called this poetry
    One of the fragile, mighty things of God,
    That die at an insult.

OLDEST PUPIL [*to other Pupils*]. Give me some true answer.
    Upon that day he spoke about the Court
    And called it the first comely child of the world,
    And said that all that was insulted there
    The world insulted, for the Courtly life
    Is the world's model. How shall I answer him?
    Can you not give me some true argument?
    I will not tempt him with a lying one.

YOUNGEST PUPIL. O, tell him that the lovers of his music
    Have need of him.

SEANCHAN. But I am labouring
　　For some that shall be born in the nick o' time,
　　And find sweet nurture, that they may have voices,
　　Even in anger, like the strings of harps;
　　And how could they be born to majesty
　　If I had never made the golden cradle?

YOUNGEST PUPIL [*throwing himself at Seanchan's feet*].
　　Why did you take me from my father's fields?
　　If you would leave me now, what shall I love?
　　Where shall I go? What shall I set my hand to?
　　And why have you put music in my ears,
　　If you would send me to the clattering houses?
　　I will throw down the trumpet and the harp,
　　For how could I sing verses or make music
　　With none to praise me, and a broken heart?

SEANCHAN. What was it that the poets promised you,
　　If it was not their sorrow? Do not speak.
　　Have I not opened school on these bare steps,
　　And are you not the youngest of my scholars?
　　And I would have all know that when all falls
　　In ruin, poetry calls out in joy,
　　Being the scattering hand, the bursting pod,
　　The victim's joy among the holy flame,
　　God's laughter at the shattering of the world.
　　And now that joy laughs out, and weeps and burns
　　On these bare steps.

YOUNGEST PUPIL. O master, do not die!

OLDEST PUPIL. Trouble him with no useless argument.
　　Be silent! There is nothing we can do
　　Except find out the King and kneel to him,
　　And beg our ancient right. For here are some
　　To say whatever we could say and more,
　　And fare as badly. Come, boy, that is no use.
　　　　[*Raises Youngest Pupil.*]
　　If it seem well that we beseech the King,
　　Lay down your harps and trumpets on the stones
　　In silence, and come with me silently.
　　Come with slow footfalls, and bow all your heads,
　　For a bowed head becomes a mourner best.

[*They lay harps and trumpets down one by one, and then go out very solemnly and slowly, following one another. Enter Mayor, two Cripples, and Brian, an old servant. The Mayor, who has been heard, before he came upon the stage, muttering 'Chief Poet', 'Ireland', etc., crosses in front of Seanchan to the other side of the steps. Brian takes food out of basket. The Cripples are watching the basket. The Mayor has an Ogham stick in his hand.*]

MAYOR [*as he crosses*]. 'Chief poet, Ireland, townsman, grazing land', those are the words I have to keep in mind, 'Chief poet, Ireland, townsman, grazing land'. I have got them all right now, they are all here cut upon the Ogham stick, 'Chief poet, Ireland, townsman, grazing land', and that's the right order.

[*He keeps muttering over his speech during what follows.*]

FIRST CRIPPLE. It would serve the King right if Seanchan drove away his luck. What's there about a king that's in the world from birth to burial like another man, that he should change old customs that were in it as long as the world has been a world?

SECOND CRIPPLE. If I were the King I wouldn't meddle with him; there is something queer about a man that makes rhymes. I knew a man that would be making rhymes year in year out under a thorn at the crossing of three roads, and he was no sooner dead than every thorn-tree from Inchy to Kiltartan withered, and he a ragged man like ourselves.

FIRST CRIPPLE. Those that make rhymes have a power from beyond the world.

MAYOR. I am getting ready.

FIRST CRIPPLE. Was it he that told you about the blessed well? And the little holy fish?

MAYOR. Hush! Hush!

SECOND CRIPPLE. It was he surely.

FIRST CRIPPLE. And it rising up out of the blessed well to cure the crippled.

SECOND CRIPPLE. Rising up every seventh year.

MAYOR. I'm half ready now.

BRIAN. There's not a mischief I begrudge the King, if it were any other man but my master—

MAYOR. Hush, I am ready.

BRIAN. That died to bring it upon him. There, I have set out the food, and if my master won't eat it, I'll home and get provision for his wake, for that's no great way off.

MAYOR. It's my turn.

BRIAN. Have your say, but don't be long about it.

MAYOR [*going close to Seanchan*]. Chief poet of Ireland, I am the Mayor of your own town, Kinvara. I am come to tell you that the news of this great trouble between you and the King of Gort has plunged us into sorrow, part for you our honoured townsman, and part for our good town. [*Begins to hesitate, scratching his head.*] But what comes after that? Something about the King.

BRIAN. Get on, the food is all set out, and maybe when you are done he'll eat a bit.

MAYOR. Don't hurry me.

FIRST CRIPPLE. Give me a taste of it, he'll not begrudge it.

SECOND CRIPPLE. Let them that have their limbs starve if they like, we have to keep in mind the stomach God has left to us.

MAYOR. Hush! I have it. The King was said to be most friendly, and we had good reason for thinking that he was about to give us those grazing lands we so much need, being so pinched that our mowers mow with knives between the stones. We asked nothing but what was reasonable. We ask you for the sake of the town to do what the King wants and then maybe he'll do what we want; we ask nothing but what's reasonable.

SEANCHAN. Reason, O reason in plenty. Yet you have yellowy white hair and not too many teeth. How comes it that you have been so long in the world and not found reason out?

[*While saying this he has turned half round; he hardly looks at the Mayor.*]

BRIAN [*trying to pull Mayor away*]. What's the good in saying all that, haven't they been reasoning with him all day long? No wonder he is tired of it. I have set the food before him ready.

MAYOR [*shoving Brian away*]. Don't hurry me. It's small respect you are showing to the town. Get further off. [*To Seanchan.*] We would not have you think, weighty as these considerations are, that they have been as weighty in our minds as our desire that one we take so much pride in, a man that is an honour to our town should live and prosper. Therefore we beseech you to give way in what is after all a matter of no importance, a matter of mere sentiment, that we may always keep our pride in you.

[*He finishes this speech with a pompous air, motions to Brian to bring the food, and sits on seat.*]

BRIAN. Master, eat this, it's not king's food that's cooked for every body and nobody. Here's barley-bread out of your father's oven and dulse from Duras. Here is the dulse, your honour, it is wholesome, it has the good taste of the sea. [*Takes dulse in one hand and bread in the other and presses them into Seanchan's hands. Seanchan shows by his movements his different feeling to Brian.*]

FIRST CRIPPLE. He has taken it and there will be nothing left.

SECOND CRIPPLE. He wanted his own sort. What's honey to a cat corn to a dog, or a green apple to a ghost in a churchyard?

SEANCHAN [*pressing food back into Brian's hands*]. Eat it yourself old man, you have come a long journey and, it may be, ate nothing on the road.

BRIAN. How could I eat it and your honour starving? It is your father that sends it. He cried because the stiffness that is in his bones prevented him coming, and he bade me tell you that he is old and has need of you, that the people will be pointing at him, that he will not be able to lift up his head if you turn the King's favour away, that he cared you well and you in your young age, and that it's right you should care him now.

SEANCHAN. What did my mother say?

BRIAN. Your mother gave no message, for when they told her that you had it in mind to starve or get again the ancient right of the poets, she said, 'No message will do any good. We cannot change him,' and she went indoors, lay down upon the bed and turned her face out of the light. [*A pause.*] Here's pigeons' eggs from Duras, and these were laid by your own hens.

SEANCHAN. She sent no message. Our mothers know us, they knew us before birth, and that is why they know us even better than sweet-hearts upon whose breasts we have lain. Tell them that my mother was in the right, go tell them that, go tell them that she knew me.

MAYOR. What is he saying? I never understood a poet's talk more than the baa of a sheep. [*Comes over from seat. Seanchan turns away.*] You have not heard, it may be, having been so much away, how many cattle died last winter from lacking grass, how much sickness there was because the poor had nothing but salt fish to live on through the winter.

BRIAN. Get away and leave the place to me, for your sack's empty.

MAYOR. Is it get away? Is that the way I'm to be spoken to? Am I not the Mayor? Am I not in authority? Am I not in the King's place? Answer me that.

BRIAN. Then show the people what a king is like; root up old customs, old habits, old rights.

MAYOR. Holy Saint Colman!

FIRST CRIPPLE. That's what the King does, and that's what you'd like to do.

SECOND CRIPPLE. Foul the holy well.

FIRST CRIPPLE. Roast the lucky fish.

SECOND CRIPPLE. Put it into your own stomach, and it meant to cure cripples.

MAYOR. How dare you take his name into your mouth, how dare you lift up your voice against the King?

BRIAN. How dare you praise him? I will have nobody praise him or any other king that robs my master.

MAYOR. And hadn't he the right to? And hadn't he the right to strike your master's head off, being the King? Or your head, or my head! I say, Long live the King! because he didn't take our heads from us. Call out long life for him.

BRIAN. IS it cry out for him?

[*The five following speeches should be spoken in a rhythmical chant, or should rise into song.*]

There's nobody'll call out for him,
But smiths will turn their anvils,
The millers turn their wheels,
The farmers turn their churns,
The witches turn their thumbs,
Till he be broken and splintered into pieces.

MAYOR. He might, if he'd a mind to it,
Be digging out our tongues,
Or dragging out our hair,
Or bleaching us like calves,
Or weaning us like lambs,
But for the kindness and the softness that is in him.

FIRST CRIPPLE. The curse of the poor be upon him,
The curse of the widows upon him,
The curse of the children upon him,
The curse of the bishops upon him,
Until he be as rotten as an old mushroom!

SECOND CRIPPLE. The curse of wrinkles be upon him!
  Wrinkles where his eyes are,
  Wrinkles where his nose is,
  Wrinkles where his mouth is,
  And a little old devil looking out of every wrinkle!

BRIAN. And nobody will sing for him,
  And nobody will hunt for him,
  And nobody will fish for him,
  And nobody will pray for him,
  But ever and always curse him and abuse him.

MAYOR. I say, Long live the King.

[*Brian seizes the Mayor.*]

  Help! Help!

BRIAN: That's how I shout for the King.

MAYOR. Help! Help! Am I not in the King's place, am I not in authority?

BRIAN. So you are—so you are. That's why I've got a hold of you.

FIRST CRIPPLE. We're teaching the King to be kind to the poor.

MAYOR. Help! Help! Wait till we're in Kinvara!

FIRST CRIPPLE [*beating the Mayor on the legs with his crutch*].
  I'll beat the royalty out of his legs.

[*The Chamberlain comes down steps shouting*, 'Silence! silence! silence!']

CHAMBERLAIN. How dare you make this uproar at the doors,
  Deafening the very greatest in the land,
  As if the farmyards and the rookeries
  Had all been emptied!

FIRST CRIPPLE. It is the Chamberlain.

[Cripples go out.]

CHAMBERLAIN. Pick up the litter there, and get you gone!
    Be quick about it! Have you no respect
    For this worn stair, this all but sacred door,
    Where suppliants and tributary kings
    Have passed, and the world's glory knelt in silence?
    Have you no reverence for what all other men
    Hold honourable?

BRIAN. If I might speak my mind,
    I'd say the King would have his luck again
    If he would let my master have his rights.

CHAMBERLAIN. Pick up your litter! Take your noise away!
    Make haste, and get the clapper from the bell!

BRIAN [*putting last of food into basket*]. What do the great and
      powerful care for rights
    That have no armies?

        [*Chamberlain begins shoving them out with his staff.*]

MAYOR. My lord, I am not to blame.
    I'm the King's man, and they attacked me for it.

BRIAN. We have our prayers, our curses and our prayers,
    And we can give a great name or a bad one.

    [*Mayor is shoving Brian out before him with one hand. He keeps his face to
    Chamberlain, and keeps bowing. The Chamberlain shoves him with his staff.*]

MAYOR. We could not make the poet eat, my lord.

        [*Chamberlain shoves him with his staff.*]

    Much honoured [*is shoved again*]—honoured to speak with you, my lord;
    But I'll go find the girl that he's to marry.
    She's coming, but I'll hurry her, my lord.
    Between ourselves, my lord [*is shoved again*], she is a great coaxer.
    Much honoured, my lord. O, she's the girl to do it;
    For when the intellect is out, my lord,
    Nobody but a woman's any good.

        [*Is shoved again.*]

    Much honoured, my lord [*is shoved again*], much honoured, much honoured!

        [*Is shoved out, shoving Brian out before him.*]

[*All through this scene, from the outset of the quarrel, Seanchan has kept his face turned away, or hidden in his cloak. While the Chamberlain has been speaking, the Soldier and the Monk have come out of the palace. The Monk stands on top of steps at one side, Soldier a little down steps at the other side. Court Ladies are seen at opening in the palace curtain behind Soldier. Chamberlain is in the centre.*]

CHAMBERLAIN [*to Seanchan*], Well, you must be contented, for your work
    Has roused the common sort against the King,
    And stolen his authority. The State
    Is like some orderly and reverend house
    Wherein, the master being dead of a sudden,
    The servants quarrel where they have a mind to,
    And pilfer here and there.

[*Pause, finding that Seanchan does not answer.*]

    How many days
    Will you keep up this quarrel with the King,
    And the King's nobles, and myself, and all,
    who'd gladly be your friends, if you would let them?

[*Going near to Monk.*]

    If you would try, you might persuade him, father.
    I cannot make him answer me, and yet,
    If fitting hands would offer him the food,
    He might accept it.

MONK. Certainly I will not.
    I've made too many homilies, wherein
    The wanton imagination of the poets
    Has been condemned, to be his flatterer.
    If pride and disobedience are unpunished
    Who will obey?

CHAMBERLAIN [*going to other side towards Soldier*].
    If you would speak to him,
    You might not find persuasion difficult,
    With all the devils of hunger helping you.

SOLDIER. I will not interfere, and if he starve
    For being obstinate and stiff in the neck,
    'Tis but good riddance.

CHAMBERLAIN. One of us must do it.
    It might be, if you'd reason with him, ladies,
    He would eat something, for I have a notion
    That if he brought misfortune on the King,
    Or the King's house, we'd be as little thought of
    As summer linen when the winter's come.

FIRST GIRL. But it would be the greater compliment If Peter'd do it.

SECOND GIRL. Reason with him, Peter.
    Persuade him to eat; he's such a bag of bones!

SOLDIER. I'll never trust a woman's word again!
    There's nobody that was so loud against him
    When he was at the council; now the wind's changed,
    And you that could not bear his speech or his silence
    Would have him there in his old place again;
    I do believe you would, but I won't help you.

SECOND GIRL. Why will you be so hard upon us, Peter?
    You know we have turned the common sort against us,
    And he looks miserable.

FIRST GIRL. We cannot dance.
    Because no harper will pluck a string for us.

SECOND GIRL. I cannot sleep with thinking of his face.

FIRST GIRL. And I love dancing more than anything.

SECOND GIRL. Do not be hard on us; but yesterday
    A woman in the road threw stones at me.
    You would not have me stoned?

FIRST GIRL. May I not dance?

SOLDIER. I will do nothing. You have put him out,
    And now that he is out—well, leave him out.

FIRST GIRL. DO it for my sake, Peter.

SECOND GIRL. And for mine.

    [*Each girl as she speaks takes Peter's hand with her right hana stroking down his
    arm with her left. While Second Girl is stroking his arm, First Girl leaves go
    and gives him the dish.*]

SOLDIER. Well, well; but not your way. [*To Seanchan*]
    Here's meat for you.
    It has been carried from too good a table
    For men like you, and I am offering it
    Because these women have made a fool of me. [*A pause.*]
    You mean to starve? You will have none of it?
    I'll leave it there, where you can sniff the savour.
    Snuff it, old hedgehog, and unroll yourself!
    But if I were the King, I'd make you do it
    With wisps of lighted straw.

SEANCHAN. You have rightly named me.
    I lie rolled up under the ragged thorns
    That are upon the edge of those great waters
    Where all things vanish away, and I have heard
    Murmurs that are the ending of all sound.
    I am out of life; I am rolled up, and yet,
    Hedgehog although I am, I'll not unroll
    For you, King's dog! Go to the King, your master.
    Crouch down and wag your tail, for it may be
    He has nothing now against you, and I think
    The stripes of your last beating are all healed.

            [*The Soldier has drawn his sword.*]

CHAMBERLAIN [*striking up sword*]. Put up your sword, sir; put it up, I say!
    The common sort would tear you into pieces
    If you but touched him.

SOLDIER. If he's to be flattered,
    Petted, cajoled, and dandled into humour,
    We might as well have left him at the table.

           [*Goes to one side sheathing sword.*]

SEANCHAN. You must needs keep your patience yet awhile,
    For I have some few mouthfuls of sweet air
    To swallow before I have grown to be as civil
    As any other dust.

CHAMBERLAIN. You wrong us, Seanchan.
    There is none here but holds you in respect;
    And if you'd only eat out of this dish,
    The King would show how much he honours you.

           [*Bowing and smiling.*]

Who could imagine you'd so take to heart
Being driven from the council? I am certain
That you, if you will only think it over,
Will understand that it is men of law,
Leaders of the King's armies, and the like,
That should sit there.

SEANCHAN. Somebody has deceived you,
    Or maybe it was your own eyes that lied,
    In making it appear that I was driven
    From the great council. You have driven away
    The images of them that weave a dance
    By the four rivers in the mountain garden.

CHAMBERLAIN. You mean we have driven poetry away.
    But that's not altogether true, for I,
    As you should know, have written poetry.
    And often when the table has been cleared,
    And candles lighted, the King calls for me,
    And I repeat it him. My poetry
    Is not to be compared with yours; but still,
    Where I am honoured, poetry, in some measure,
    Is honoured too.

SEANCHAN. Well, if you are a poet,
    Cry out that the King's money would not buy,
    Nor the high circle consecrate his head,
    If poets had never christened gold, and even
    The moon's poor daughter, that most whey-faced metal,
    Precious; cry out that not a man alive
    Would ride among the arrows with high heart,
    Or scatter with an open hand, had not
    Our heady craft commended wasteful virtues.
    And when that story's finished, shake your coat
    Where little jewels gleam on it, and say,
    A herdsman, sitting where the pigs had trampled,
    Made up a song about enchanted kings,
    Who were so finely dressed one fancied them
    All fiery, and women by the churn
    And children by the hearth caught up the song
    And murmured it, until the tailors heard it.

CHAMBERLAIN. If you would but eat something, you'd find out
    That you have had these thoughts from lack of food,
    For hunger makes us feverish.

SEANCHAN. Cry aloud
    That when we are driven out we come again
    Like a great wind that runs out of the waste
    To blow the tables flat; and thereupon
    Lie down upon the threshold till the King
    Restore to us the ancient right of the poets.

MONK. You cannot shake him. I will to the King,
    And offer him consolation in his trouble,
    For that man there has set his teeth to die.
    He is a man that hates obedience,
    Discipline, and orderliness of life;
    I cannot mourn him.

FIRST GIRL. 'Twas you that stirred it up.
    You stirred it up that you might spoil our dancing.
    Why shouldn't we have dancing? We're not in Lent.
    Yet nobody will pipe or play to us;
    And they will never do it if he die.
    And that is why you are going.

MONK. What folly's this?

FIRST GIRL. Well, if you did not do it, speak to him—
    Use your authority; make him obey you.
    What harm is there in dancing?

MONK. Hush! begone!
    Go to the fields and watch the hurley players,
    Or any other place you have a mind to.
    This is not woman's work.

FIRST GIRL. Come! let's away!
    We can do nothing here.

MONK. The pride of the poets!
    Dancing, hurling, the country full of noise,
    And King and Church neglected. Seanchan,
    I'll take my leave, for you are perishing
    Like all that let the wanton imagination
    Carry them where it will, and it's not likely
    I'll look upon your living face again.

SEANCHAN. Come nearer, nearer!

MONK. Have you some last wish?

SEANCHAN. Stoop down, for I would whisper it in your ear.
Has that wild God of yours, that was so wild
When you'd but lately taken the King's pay,
Grown any tamer? He gave you all much trouble.

MONK. Let go my habit!

SEANCHAN. Have you persuaded him
To chirp between two dishes when the King
Sits down to table?

MONK. Let go my habit, sir!

[*Crosses to centre of stage.*]

SEANCHAN. And maybe he has learned to sing quite softly
Because loud singing would disturb the King,
Who is sitting drowsily among his friends
After the table has been cleared. Not yet!

[*Seanchan has been dragged some feet clinging to the Monk's habit.*]

You did not think that hands so full of hunger
Could hold you tightly. They are not civil yet.
I'd know if you have taught him to eat bread
From the King's hand, and perch upon his finger.
I think he perches on the King's strong hand,
But it may be that he is still too wild.
You must not weary in your work; a king
Is often weary, and he needs a God
To be a comfort to him.

[*The Monk plucks his habit away and goes into palace. Seanchan holds up his hand
as if a bird perched upon it. He pretends to stroke the bird.*]

A little God,
With comfortable feathers, and bright eyes.

FIRST GIRL. There will be no more dancing in our time. For nobody will play the harp
or the fiddle. Let us away, for we cannot amend it, And watch the hurley.

SECOND GIRL. Hush! he is looking at us.

SEANCHAN. Yes, yes, go to the hurley, go to the hurley,
 Go to the hurley! Gather up your skirts—
 Run quickly! You can remember many love songs;
 I know it by the light that's in your eyes—
 But you'll forget them. You're fair to look upon.
 Your feet delight in dancing, and your mouths
 In the slow smiling that awakens love.
 The mothers that have borne you mated rightly.
 They'd little ears as thirsty as your ears
 For many love songs. Go to the young men.
 Are not the ruddy flesh and the thin flanks
 And the broad shoulders worthy of desire?
 Go from me! Here is nothing for your eyes.
 But it is I that am singing you away—
 Singing you to the young men.

 [*The two young Princesses come out of palace. While he has been speaking the Girls
 have shrunk back holding each other's hands.*]

FIRST GIRL. Be quiet!
 Look who it is has come out of the house.
 Princesses, we are for the hurling field.
 Will you go there?

FIRST PRINCESS. We will go with you, Aileen.
 But we must have some words with Seanchan,
 For we have come to make him eat and drink.

CHABERLAIN. I will hold out the dish and cup for him
 While you are speaking to him of his folly,
 If you desire it, Princess.

 [*He has taken dish and cup.*]

FIRST PRINCESS. No, Finula
 Will carry him the dish and I the cup.
 We'll offer them ourselves.

 [*They take cup and dish.*]

FIRST GIRL. They are so gracious;
 The dear little Princesses are so gracious.

 [*Princess holds out her hand for Seanchan to kiss it. He does not move.*]

 Although she is holding out her hand to him,
 He will not kiss it.

FIRST PRINCESS. My father bids us say
    That, though he cannot have you at his table,
    You may ask any other thing you like
    And he will give it you. We carry you
    With our own hands a dish and cup of wine.

FIRST GIRL. O, look! he has taken it! He has taken it!
    The dear Princesses! I have always said
    That nobody could refuse them anything.

    [*Seanchan takes the cup in one hand. In the other he holds for a moment the hand of the Princess.*]

SEANCHAN. O, long, soft fingers and pale finger-tips,
    Well worthy to be laid in a king's hand!
    O, you have fair white hands, for it is certain
    There is uncommon whiteness in these hands.
    But there is something comes into my mind,
    Princess. A little while before your birth,
    I saw your mother sitting by the road
    In a high chair; and when a leper passed,
    She pointed him the way into the town.
    He lifted up his hand and blessed her hand—
    I saw it with my own eyes. Hold out your hands;
    I will find out if they are contaminated,
    For it has come into my thoughts that maybe
    The King has sent me food and drink by hands
    That are contaminated. I would see all your hands.
    You've eyes of dancers; but hold out your hands,
    For it may be there are none sound among you.

    [*The Princesses have shrunk back in terror.*]

FIRST PRINCESS. He has called us lepers.

    [*Soldier draws sword.*]

CHAMBERLAIN. He's out of his mind,
    And does not know the meaning of what he said.

SEANCHAN [*standing up*]. There's no sound hand among you—no sound hand.
    Away with you! away with all of you!
    You are all lepers! There is leprosy
    Among the plates and dishes that you have carried.
    And wherefore have you brought me leper's wine?

    [*He flings the contents of the cup in their faces.*]

There, there! I have given it to you again. And now
Begone, or I will give my curse to you.
You have the leper's blessing, but you think
Maybe the bread will something lack in savour
Unless you mix my curse into the dough.

[*They go out hurriedly in all directions. Seanchan is staggering in the middle of the
stage.*]

Where did I say the leprosy had come from?
I said it came out of a leper's hand,

Enter Cripples

And that he walked the highway. But that's folly,
For he was walking up there in the sky.
And there he is even now, with his white hand
Thrust out of the blue air, and blessing them
With leprosy.

FIRST CRIPPLE. He's pointing at the moon
    That's coming out up yonder, and he calls it
    Leprous, because the daylight whitens it.

SEANCHAN. He's holding up his hand above them all—
    King, noblemen, princesses—blessing all.
    Who could imagine he'd have so much patience?

FIRST CRIPPLE [*clutching the other Cripple*]. Come out of this!

SECOND CRIPPLE [*pointing to food*]. If you don't need it, sir,
    May we not carry some of it away?

[*They cross towards food and pass in front of Seanchan.*]

SEANCHAN. Who's speaking? Who are you?

FIRST CRIPPLE. Come out of this!

SECOND CRIPPLE. Have pity on us, that must beg our bread
    From table to table throughout the entire world,
    And yet be hungry.

SEANCHAN. But why were you born crooked?
    What bad poet did your mothers listen to
    That you were born so crooked?

FIRST CRIPPLE. Come away!
Maybe he's cursed the food, and it might kill us.

SECOND CRIPPLE. Yes, better come away. [*They go out.*]

SEANCHAN [*staggering and speaking wearily*].
He has great strength
And great patience to hold his right hand there,
Uplifted, and not wavering about.
He is much stronger than I am, much stronger.

[*Sinks down on steps. Mayor and Fedelm have entered.*]

MAYOR. He is delirious now.

FEDELM. Before I speak
Of food or drink I'll take him out of this.
For while he is on this threshold and can hear,
It may be, the voices that made mock of him,
He would not listen.

MAYOR. No, speak to him at once.
Press food upon him while delirious
And he may eat not knowing what he does. [*Mayor goes out.*]

FEDELM. Seanchan! Seanchan!

[*He remains looking into the sky.*]

Can you not hear me, Seanchan?
It is myself.

[*He looks at her, dreamily at first, then takes her hand.*]

SEANCHAN. Is this your hand, Fedelm?
I have been looking at another hand
That is up yonder.

FEDELM. I have come for you.

SEANCHAN. Fedelm, I did not know that you were here.

FEDELM. And can you not remember that I promised
That I would come and take you home with me
When I'd the harvest in? And now I've come,
And you must come away, and come on the instant.

SEANCHAN. Yes, I will come. But is the harvest in?
  This air has got a summer taste in it.

FEDELM. But is not the wild middle of the summer
  A better time to marry? Come with me now!

SEANCHAN [*seizing her by both wrists*]. Who taught you that?
  For it's a certainty,
  Although I never knew it till last night,
  That marriage, because it is the height of life,
  Can only be accomplished to the full
  In the high days of the year. I lay awake:
  There had come a frenzy into the light of the stars,
  And they were coming nearer, and I knew
  All in a minute they were about to marry
  Clods out upon the ploughlands, to beget
  A mightier race than any that has been.
  But some that are within there made a noise,
  And frighted them away.

FEDELM. Come with me now!
  We have far to go, and daylight's running out.

SEANCHAN. The stars had come so near me that I caught
  Their singing. It was praise of that great race
  That would be haughty, mirthful, and white-bodied,
  With a high head, and open hand, and how,
  Laughing, it would take the mastery of the world.

FEDELM. But you will tell me all about their songs
  When we're at home. You have need of rest and care,
  And I can give them you when we're at home.
  And therefore let us hurry, and get us home.

SEANCHAN. It's certain that there is some trouble here,
  Although it's gone out of my memory.
  And I would get away from it. Give me your help.

                    [*Trying to rise.*]

  But why are not my pupils here to help me?
  Go, call my pupils, for I need their help.

FEDELM. Come with me now, and I will send for them
 For I have a great room that's full of beds
 I can make ready; and there is a smooth lawn
 Where they can play at hurley and sing poems
 Under an apple-tree.

SEANCHAN. I know that place:
 An apple-tree, and a smooth level lawn
 Where the young men can sway their hurley sticks. [*Sings*]
  The four rivers that run there,
  Through well-mown level ground,
  Have come out of a blessed well
  That is all bound and wound
  By the great roots of an apple
  And all the fowls of the air
  Have gathered in the wide branches
  And keep singing there.

   [*Fedelm, troubled, has covered her eyes with her hands.*]

FEDELM. No, there are not four rivers, and those rhymes
 Praise Adam's paradise.

SEANCHAN. I can remember now,
 It's out of a poem I made long ago
 About the Garden in the East of the World
 And how spirits in the images of birds
 Crowd in the branches of old Adam's crab-tree.
 They come before me now, and dig in the fruit
 With so much gluttony, and are so drunk
 With that harsh wholesome savour, that their feathers
 Are clinging one to another with the juice.
 But you would lead me to some friendly place,
 And I would go there quickly.

FEDELM [*helping him to rise*]. Come with me.

   [*He walks slowly, supported by her, till he comes to table.*]

SEANCHAN. But why am I so weak? Have I been ill?
 Sweetheart, why is it that I am so weak? [*Sinks on to seat.*]

FEDELM [*goes to table*]. I'll dip this piece of bread into the wine,
 For that will make you stronger for the journey.

SEANCHAN. Yes, give me bread and wine; that's what I want,
 For it is hunger that is gnawing me.

[*He takes bread from Fedelm, hesitates, and then thrusts it back into her hand. But no; I must not eat it.*]

FEDELM. Eat, Seanchan,
    For if you do not eat it you will die.

SEANCHAN. Why did you give me food? Why did you come?
    For had I not enough to fight against
    Without your coming?

FEDELM. Eat this little crust,
    Seanchan, if you have any love for me.

SEANCHAN. I must not eat it—but that's beyond your wit.
    Child! child! I must not eat it, though I die.

FEDELM [*passionately*]. You do not know what love is; for if you loved,
    You would put every other thought away.
    But you have never loved me.

SEANCHAN [*seizing her by wrist*].
    You, a child,
    Who have but seen a man out of the window,
    Tell me that I know nothing about love,
    And that I do not love you? Did I not say
    There was a frenzy in the light of the stars
    All through the livelong night, and that the night
    Was full of marriages? But that fight's over
    And all that's done with, and I have to die.

FEDELM [*throwing her arms about him*]. I will not be put from you, although I think
    I had not grudged it you if some great lady,
    If the King's daughter, had set out your bed.
    I will not give you up to death; no, no!
    And are not these white arms and this soft neck
    Better than the brown earth?

SEANCHAN [*struggling to disengage himself*]. Begone from me!
    There's treachery in those arms and in that voice.
    They're all against me. Why do you linger there?
    How long must I endure the sight of you?

FEDELM. O, Seanchan! Seanchan!

SEANCHAN [rising]. Go where you will,
 So it be out of sight and out of mind.
 I cast you from me like an old torn cap,
 A broken shoe, a glove without a finger,
 A crooked penny; whatever is most worthless.

FEDELM [*bursts into tears*]. O, do not drive me from you!

SEANCHAN [*takes her in his arms*]. What did I say,
 My dove of the woods? I was about to curse you.
 It was a frenzy. I'll unsay it all.
 But you must go away.

FEDELM. Let me be near you.
 I will obey like any married wife.
 Let me but lie before your feet.

SEANCHAN. Come nearer. [*Kisses her.*]
 If I had eaten when you bid me, sweetheart,
 The kiss of multitudes in times to come
 Had been the poorer.

   [*Enter King from palace, followed by the two Princesses.*]

KING [*to Fedelm*]. Has he eaten yet?

FEDELM. No, King, and will not till you have restored
 The right of the poets.

KING [*coming down and standing before Seanchan*]. Seanchan, have refused
 Everybody I have sent, and now
 I come to you myself.

FEDELM. Come nearer, King.
 He is now so weak he cannot hear your voice.

KING. Seanchan, put away your pride as I
 Have put my pride away. I had your love
 Not a great while ago, and now you have planned
 To put a voice by every cottage fire,
 And in the night when no one sees who cries,
 To cry against me till my throne has crumbled.
 And yet if I give way I must offend
 My courtiers and nobles till they, too,
 Strike at the crown. What would you have of me?

SEANCHAN. When did the poets promise safety, King?

KING Seanchan, I bring you bread in my own hands,
    And bid you eat because of all these reasons,
    And for this further reason, that I love you.

[*Seanchan pushes bread away, with Fedelm's hand.*]

You have refused, Seanchan?

SEANCHAN. We have refused it.

KING. I have been patient, though I am a king,
    And have the means to force you. But that's ended,
    And I am but a king, and you a subject.
    Nobles and courtiers, bring the poets hither;

[*Enter Court Ladies, Monk, Soldiers, Chamberlain, and Courtiers with Pupils, who*
    have halters round their necks.]

For you can have your way. I that was man,
    With a man's heart, am now all king again.
    Speak to your master; beg your lives of him;
    Show him the halter that is round your necks.
    If his heart's set upon it, he may die;
    But you shall all die with him. [*Goes up steps.*]
    Beg your lives!
    Begin, for you have little time to lose.
    Begin it, you that are the oldest pupil.

OLDEST PUPIL. Die, Seanchan, and proclaim the right of the poets.

KING. Silence! you are as crazy as your master.
    But that young boy, that seems the youngest of you,
    I'd have him speak. Kneel down before him, boy;
    Hold up your hands to him that you may pluck
    That milky-coloured neck out of the noose.

YOUNGEST PUPIL. Die, Seanchan, and proclaim the right of the poets.

SEANCHAN. Come nearer me that I may know how face
    Differs from face and touch you with my hands.
    O more than kin, O more than children could be,
    For children are but born out of our blood
    And share our frailty. O my chicks, my chicks!
    That I have nourished underneath my wings
    And fed upon my soul. [*He rises and walks down steps.*]
    I need no help.
    He needs no help that joy has lifted up

Like some miraculous beast out of Ezekiel.
The man that dies has the chief part in the story,
And I will mock and mock that image yonder,
That evil picture in the sky—no, no!
I have all my strength again, I will outface it.
O, look upon the moon that's standing there
In the blue daylight—take note of the complexion,
Because it is the white of leprosy
And the contagion that afflicts mankind
Falls from the moon. When I and these are dead
We should be carried to some windy hill
To lie there with uncovered face awhile
That mankind and that leper there may know
Dead faces laugh. [*He falls and then half rises.*]
King! King! Dead faces laugh. [*He dies.*]

OLDEST PUPIL. King, he is dead; some strange triumphant thought
So filled his heart with joy that it has burst,
Being grown too mighty for our frailty,
And we who gaze grow like him and abhor
The moments that come between us and that death
You promised us.

KING. Take up his body.
Go where you please and lay it where you please,
So that I cannot see his face or any
That cried him towards his death.

YOUNGEST PUPIL. Dead faces laugh!
The ancient right is gone, the new remains,
And that is death.

[*They go towards the King holding out their halters.*]

We are impatient men,
So gather up the halters in your hands.

KING. Drive them away.

[*He goes into the palace. The Soldiers block the way before the Pupils.*]

SOLDIER. Here is no place for you,
For he and his pretensions now are finished.
Begone before the men-at-arms are bidden
To beat you from the door.

OLDEST PUPIL. Take up his body
  And cry that, driven from the populous door,
  He seeks high waters and the mountain birds
  To claim a portion of their solitude.

  [*They make a litter with cloak and staffs or use one discovered, heaped with food, at
      the opening of the play.*]

YOUNGEST PUPIL. And cry that when they took his ancient right
  They took all common sleep; therefore he claims
  The mountain for his mattress and his pillow.

OLDEST PUPIL. And there he can sleep on, not noticing,
  Although the world be changed from worse to worse,
  Amid the changeless clamour of the curlew.

  [*They raise the litter on their shoulders and move a few steps.*]

YOUNGEST PUPIL [*motioning to them to stop*].
  Yet make triumphant music; sing aloud,
  For coming times will bless what he has blessed
  And curse what he has cursed.

OLDEST PUPIL. No, no, be still,
  Or pluck a solemn music from the strings.
  You wrong his greatness speaking so of triumph.

YOUNGEST PUPIL. O silver trumpets, be you lifted up
  And cry to the great race that is to come.
  Long-throated swans upon the waves of time,
  Sing loudly, for beyond the wall of the world
  That race may hear our music and awake.

OLDEST PUPIL [*motioning the musicians to lower their trumpets*].
  Not what it leaves behind it in the light
  But what it carries with it to the dark
  Exalts the soul; nor song nor trumpet-blast
  Can call up races from the worsening world
  To mend the wrong and mar the solitude
  Of the great shade we follow to the tomb.

  [*Fedelm and the Pupils go out carrying the litter. Some play a Mournful music.*]

THE END

.

CPSIA information can be obtained at www.ICGtesting.com
Printed in the USA
BVOW08s1303060214

344026BV00002B/523/P